HOW TO TAKE THE FOG OUT OF BUSINESS WRITING

By Robert Gunning

and Richard A. Kallan

ILLUSTRATIONS BY STEVE MEEK

DARTNELL is a publisher serving the world of business with books, manuals, newsletters and bulletins, and training materials for executives, managers, supervisors, salespeople, financial officials, personnel executives, and office employees. Dartnell also produces management and sales training videos and audiocassettes, publishes many useful business forms, and many of its materials and films are available in languages other than English. Dartnell, established in 1917, serves the world's business community. For details, catalogs, and product information, write to:

THE DARTNELL CORPORATION,
4660 N Ravenswood Ave,
Chicago, IL 60640-4595, U.S.A.
or phone (800) 621-5463, in U.S. and Canada.

Dartnell Training Limited
125 High Holborn
London, England
WC1V 6QA
or phone 011-44-071-404-1585

This publication is designed to provide accurate and authoritative information in regard to the subject matter covered. It is sold with the understanding that the publisher is not engaged in rendering legal, accounting, or other professional service. If legal advice or other expert assistance is required, the services of a competent professional person should be sought.

—From a Declaration of Principles jointly adopted by a Committee of the American Bar Association and a Committee of Publishers.

ISBN 0–85013–232–0

Library of Congress Catalog Card Number: 94-79092

Printed in the United States of America by the Dartnell Press, Chicago, IL 60640-4595

CONTENTS   PAGE

THE DARTNELL CORPORATION
CHICAGO, IL 60640-4595

*Fog Index^{SM} is a service mark licensed exclusively to
RK Communication Consultants by D. and M. Mueller.

INTRODUCTION

The clear writing ideas developed by Robert Gunning and Richard A. Kallan can save time, money, and energy for any business or organization. The explanations given are crisp, concise, and easy to apply. Just 10 minutes of editing and rewriting can bring any stuffy writing to life, making it more interesting, readable, and *effective*.

Such editing is needed desperately. While many businesses are efficient in production, marketing, and research, business writing lags behind, often neglected. And, yet, bad business writing surely drains profits. No company can afford it.

How to Take the Fog Out of Business Writing shows you how to remedy the situation. It introduces you to the 10 Principles of Clear Statement; it offers 24 simple ways to improve writing; and it describes how to use the Fog Index[SM] scale to measure the complexity of your writing.

The ideas presented were inspired by Robert Gunning (1908-1980). One of the founders of the clear writing movement in the 1940s, Gunning developed a way to coach the staffs of such newspapers as *The Wall Street Journal* to write for experts and nonexperts alike. In 1944, he invented the famed Fog Index[SM] scale, an easy way to measure the complexity of prose. Later, he turned to business and conducted clear writing seminars for hundreds of corporations, including more than 100 Fortune 500 companies.

Richard A. Kallan received his Ph.D. in communication studies from Northwestern University. For more than 20 years, Kallan has taught writing and speaking as a management consultant and as a professor for such institutions as the Graduate

School of Business at the University of Southern California and in the Writing Program at the University of California, Santa Barbara. In 1993, he became director of the Robert Gunning Clear Writing Institute in Santa Barbara, California.

Author's Note

This new edition of *How to Take the Fog Out of Business Writing* reflects the most significant revision since the book was first published in 1956.

I have modified, updated, and expanded the previous (1985) work. Most noticeably, a new section — "The 18 Most Commonly Asked Questions About Business Writing" — has been added.

Still, the basic outline and intent of the original text remain the same. There seemed little reason to overhaul what nearly 800,000 readers have welcomed: a *clear* book about writing clearly. Indeed, the "10 Principles of Clear Statement," the Fog Index[SM] scale, and "24 Ways to Lift *Fog*" are as fresh and relevant today as they were nearly 40 years ago.

The changes made in the present edition benefited from the sage counsel of three individuals: Darla Anderson, Al Melkonian, and Douglas Mueller. To each, I am indebted.

Richard A. Kallan

Santa Barbara, California, 1994

The High Cost of Poor Writing

Poor writing is very costly. Just how costly? Consider these common scenarios:

- *An unclear letter* so confuses the reader that it requires "corrective" correspondence, resulting in lost time, more work, and a strained relationship.

- *An imprecise memo* spurs the opposite action intended, thus wasting precious resources and misdirecting corporate focus.

- *A poorly organized report* with unclear structure and inadequately developed information results in vital facts going unnoticed.

- *A long and ponderous proposal* for needed action is set aside because it's unreadable.

- *A major presentation prepared carelessly* by subordinates forces a senior executive to spend hours editing and rewriting.

Add to these scenarios the cost of extra paper, ink, copying, and postage — as well as additional administrative support, computer use, and telephone/fax expense. They add up to billions of dollars wasted every year because of poor writing.

The culprit in most bad writing is *fog*, our code word for *unnecessary* complexity. On page after page of this book, we show how widely *fog* exists

Fortunately, *fog* can be avoided. We point the way by showing how to detect and eliminate it. Using actual examples, we also illustrate frequent faults of business writing, many of which contribute to *fog*.

*Skill in writing comes only after long practice.
But the first giant step toward improvement can
be taken quickly and easily. Let's begin.*

FOG . . . AND WHY IT OCCURS

Fog arises from frozen phrases and windy expressions. Unlike the spoken word, *fogged* prose never sounds natural.

Did you ever hear anyone *say*:

We are in receipt of your correspondence and will initiate an appropriate corrective response. . . .

Kindly advise if your information gives confirmation to the conclusions herein outlined. . . .

Given the primary objectives of optimum utilization, it was deemed advisable that . . .

Just reading such language is taxing. Unless we're comedians or satirists, most of us don't speak this way.

You must avoid such pomposity if you truly care about your reader. And you can, if you commit to the Writer's Golden Rule: *Write unto others as you want others to write unto you.*

Fog exists because writers fail to ask themselves the right questions — the same questions they're quick to pose in the laboratory, factory, and office.

• Precisely what are we doing?

• How can we do it better today than yesterday?

• How can we make it more useful, in less time, and with less effort and expense?

Such questions have always been asked by leaders in business, research, and government.

When it comes to writing, however, the past is enshrined. Watch a colleague start a major report or proposal. (Perhaps you have done this yourself.) The first question is: *How did we do this the last time?*

Before starting, most business writers check the files to get examples of earlier reports and proposals. When they find a tried-and-true form that promises to save them time and energy, the allure proves irresistible. That's why today's business writing perpetuates so many bad habits of decades past.

TEN PRINCIPLES OF CLEAR STATEMENT

Although we've talked to scores of people about writing, we've yet to find anyone completely confident about *how* to do it. Ironically, many superb writers are the most humble. Because they recognize the scope and power of language, they feel their prose never quite reaches its full potential.

Regrettably, much writing advice — like that on the fine points of grammar — sheds little light on how to produce clear communication. Writing is an art that can't be encased in a set of *rules*. Rules replace thought; without thinking, you can't write well.

Effective writing requires, instead of rules, a set of *principles* — some guidelines that strike at the source of *fog*.

Our 10 Principles of Clear Statement address that goal. They serve to guide clear thinking and thereby produce clear writing:

1. KEEP SENTENCES SHORT — ON THE AVERAGE.

For easy reading, sentences should vary in structure and length, but the *average* should be short — between 15 and 20 words. In popular publications, sentence length varies from two or three words to 30 or more, yet the average is below 20.

2. PREFER THE SIMPLE TO THE COMPLEX.

This doesn't mean you should forever avoid using complex words or phrases. You need both simple and complex forms to express ideas clearly. If the right word is a long one, use it. But if a shorter word can do the job, use it. Write "try to find out," rather than "endeavor to ascertain." Remember to ask: *Why am I using the longer word? Do I really need it?*

3. Develop your vocabulary.

Don't let your preference for short words limit your vocabulary. The more words you know — short and long — the more precise your writing. A poor vocabulary confines your thinking and impairs your expression.

4. Avoid unneeded words.

Nothing weakens writing more than verbosity: It tires the text and slows the reader. Scrutinize your own writing to make sure every word carries its weight. Practice shaving needless words, even when you draft personal notes and letters. Sometimes you can cut as much as half of your [~~written~~] prose.

5. Keep action in your verbs.

The dreariness of most business writing comes from overusing passive verbs. Active verbs bring writing to life by streamlining sentences and emphasizing action. They also make writing sound more conversational: "We intend to write clearly," not "Clarity of composition is our intention."

6. Write the way you speak.

When you catch yourself writing a long or awkward phrase, ask yourself: *How would I say it if the reader were sitting across the desk?* A clear, conversational tone — using "we" and "you" freely, for example — is more readable than a style filled with business jargon.

7. Use concrete language.

Winston Churchill told his wartime parliament: "I have nothing to offer but blood, toil, tears, and sweat." His vivid language stirred a nation to new hope. Abstract words can render writing dull and obtuse. Select short, concrete words your reader can visualize.

8. Relate to your reader's experience.

The reader won't accept new ideas unless they're linked to older, more acceptable experiences. Carefully choose words that appeal to your audience's unique mind-set. Words don't have fixed meanings. For each person, the meaning of any word includes those personal experiences associated with it.

9. Vary your style.

Keep your writing fresh and interesting by varying your sentence structure, sentence length, and vocabulary. Avoid repetitive patterns that call attention to themselves. Even short sentences, when used exclusively, can produce a "choppy," distracting effect.

10. Write to Express, not to Impress.

Most business writing suffers from the writer's desire to *sound* knowledgeable and confident. As a result, needless complexity rules the page. The truly impressive writer is one who can express complex ideas in clear, simple terms.

HOW TO USE THE FOG INDEX^{SM} SCALE

In the 1920s, educators began developing readability yardsticks to measure writing complexity. They showed how tabulations of sentence length and specific word use could predict whether readers would understand a written passage. Early readability formulas, however, were too complicated and tedious for practical use.

In 1944, Robert Gunning developed a simple, quick, and reliable way to measure writing complexity, called the Fog Index^{SM} scale.

The Fog Index^{SM} score represents the approximate years of schooling needed to comprehend a piece of writing. The higher the Fog Index^{SM} score, the harder the writing is to read.

FINDING YOUR FOG INDEX^{SM} SCORE:

Pick a writing sample of at least 100 words, ending with a period. Then, follow these steps:

1. Figure the average number of words per sentence. Treat independent clauses (word groupings within a sentence that could stand alone) as separate sentences. Example: "We studied; we learned; we improved." Such statements should be counted as three sentences, even when commas, semicolons, or dashes are used instead of periods to separate the clauses. Hyphenated words ("twenty-five"), numbers ("25"), and dates ("1994") count as one word. (December 25, 1994 = three words.)

2. Count the words of three syllables or more. Don't count capitalized words, including the first word of each sentence; combinations of short, easy words, like "bookkeeper," "butter-

fly," or "pawnbroker"; or verbs made into three syllables by adding *-ed* or *-es* (such as "created" or "trespasses"). Divide the count by the word length of your writing sample to determine the percentage of long (polysyllabic) words. Example: Sixteen long words in a 130-word sample = 12.3%.

3. Add #1 (average sentence length = 14) to #2 (percentage of long words = 12.3). **Total** = 26.3. The Fog Index[SM] score equals 26.3 x 0.4 equals 10.52, or 10. (Drop the digits after the decimal point.)

Note: Few readers have more than 17 years of schooling, so any passage above 17 gets a Fog Index[SM] score of 17+.

Beware: Don't try to write by this or any formula. To write clearly, apply the 10 Principles of Clear Statement. Then test the complexity of your writing occasionally, using the Fog Index[SM] scale on a variety of samples. If your score consistently exceeds 12, you're handicapping your copy — and your readers.

Putting the Fog Index^{SM} Scale to Work

At the left are samples of typical business writing. The revisions at the right show how their Fog Index^{SM} scores — and lengths — can be cut:

Fog Index^{SM} Score 12

It has been the practice of the company, in most overseas markets, to lend various amounts of money to dealers for the reconstruction of existing retail outlets. Up to the present, the total amount loaned for this purpose is about $100 million.

Fog Index^{SM} Score 4

In most overseas markets, we have loaned money to dealers to rebuild retail stores. These loans total about $100 million.

Fog Index^{SM} Score 17+

Despite the fact that the time required for the improvement of one's writing skills may seem excessive at the beginning, it will pay dividends in the long run, for once a reasonable degree of skill in writing is achieved, it will be apparent that the time needed in the future to write will be appreciably less.

Fog Index^{SM} Score 6

At first it will seem to take forever to improve your writing skills. However, your investment will pay off: Your future writing will need much less effort.

Fog Index^{SM} Score 14

Results obtained from the torsion test indicated that two months of aging of the rubber had no apparent effect on its elastic properties. There was no significant change in the results of the test on the original rubber and on the rubber after two months of aging.

Fog Index^{SM} Score 11

The torsion test showed that aging the rubber for two months had no apparent effect on its elasticity.

Too many of us write for the record instead of for the reader. Keeping a thorough record is, no doubt, important. Still, even the most replete document is useless unless it can be understood.

Before you write, ask yourself, *What do people actually read?* Most of us could read *anything* if we had to. Yet, because competition for our time is so great, we tend to skip pages heavy with *fog*.

Our choice of magazines tells the story. Of those that depend on text for their circulation, here's how some rate on the Fog Index^{SM} scale:

Reader's Digest 10

Time, Newsweek 11

Harper's, Atlantic 12

Harper's and *Atlantic* are literary magazines aimed at college-educated readers. Nevertheless, both magazines have a Fog Index^{SM} score at the high-school senior level. Why? Because people prefer easier reading.

Would you want *your* writing to be more difficult than that of *Harper's* or *Atlantic*? Probably not. Yet studies of corporate prose show that memos, letters, and reports are more complicated than these popular magazines.

Good writing remains free from needless complexity. Most best-selling books have a Fog Index^{SM} score of 8 to 10. The Bible, for the most part, tests 6 and 7.

24 WAYS TO LIFT *FOG*

The Fog Index^{SM} scale is handy for judging readability, but it's not a "cookie cutter." You haven't written clearly just because your Fog Index^{SM} score is low. Anyone can throw together a bunch of short-worded, short sentences that says nothing.

To write clearly, first apply the 10 Principles of Clear Statement (pp 12-15), then use the Fog Index^{SM} scale to gauge what you've written.

To further fight *fog*, learn to spot writing faults. Twenty-four typical faults of business writers are analyzed on the pages that follow. Each is discussed and illustrated, followed by tips on how to avoid or correct the problem.

All our examples are real. They were written by competent employees from large companies and organizations. In a few instances, the authors were top executives. (To conceal identities, we slightly changed most examples.)

Our purpose isn't to belittle these writers. We merely wish to show that good writing is hard work. Not surprisingly, anyone can miss the mark.

FAULT #1: MARATHON SENTENCES

A busy sales manager writes:

I would appreciate it very much if when there are any future occasions to call matters of this type to my attention, that the memo be addressed to the Order Department, with a copy sent to me, rather than sending it directly to me, which calls for separate attention, and which would then allow me to see that compliance is secured with equal effectiveness (if the case is so noted by copy to the appropriate department or person).

What is meant by that 78-word monstrosity?

The manager would have been understood more easily had he or she simply tightened the reins on this otherwise runaway sentence. Less than *half* as many words, broken into two sentences, would have done the job:

Please address future memos of this sort to the Order Department, with a copy sent to me. In this way, I can attend to the matter without writing an additional memo.

It's possible to write long, *readable* sentences. But they're best left to highly skilled writers. Charles Dickens, Thomas Wolfe, and Ernest Hemingway, now and then, wrote sentences of 100 words or more. Yet, even these accomplished authors did so only occasionally. On the average, their sentences were fewer than 20 words.

Sentence length in such popular magazines as *Time* and *Reader's Digest* varies considerably. But the *average* sentence length, issue after issue, is 15–20 words.

Cure: Break Them Up

Break up long sentences if you want to keep your message clear. Remember that when you speak you usually give *one* idea at a time. And you pause for emphasis.

Even a good writer can get lost in the maze of a marathon sentence. The following example was written by a lawyer for a manufacturing firm. The sentence was so important that it was reproduced and sent to dozens of salespeople. They, in turn, included it in their letters. Because the sentence was so long, however, no one noticed that it didn't say what the writer intended:

Orders for machines and equipment are accepted with the understanding that they will be invoiced at prices in effect at the time of shipment, but any applicable increase not to exceed 15 percent of the total price of the order as accepted, provided delivery can be completed within 15 months from date of acceptance.

The error would have been evident to anyone who wrote and copied this paragraph — if the sentence hadn't been so long. Once you break the sentence in two, you see at once the absence of an all-important "is" after the word "increase."

Orders for machines and equipment are accepted with the understanding that they will be invoiced at prices in effect at the time of shipment. However, any applicable increase is not to exceed 15 percent of the total price of the order as accepted, provided delivery can be completed within 15 months from the date of acceptance.

Watch for marathon sentences in your writing. Note how easily they can be broken apart. Often, you can just scratch the coordinating conjunction ("and" or "but," for example) and re-punctuate.

FAULT #2: FAILURE TO COME TO THE POINT

Suppose I had just seen the All-Star Baseball Game. You weren't able to go, so you ask, "How did the game turn out?"

"Well, it was really a great day for a game. The sun was shining, a breeze was blowing in from the outfield, and the stadium was packed. Just a perfect day for a game. I got to the ballpark early to watch —"

You interrupt, "But who won?" You want to know.

"Well, there was a big ceremony before it started. The Navy sent the Blue Angels air squadron, and the governor threw out the first ball —"

"Yes, yes, but who won? Who won??"

"I'm coming to that. The opening pitcher for the American League was Anderson, and his first pitch was right over the plate. . . ."

By this time, you're either gone or ready to take a swing at me. My way is not how to report a ball game. You first want to know who won. After that, you may be interested in details. But *first* you want the score. You want the "lead," the main idea in the message.

Too much business writing is composed as if it were a short story or one-act play. The author creates suspense, holding back the big news until the end. If you're writing to *entertain*, that may be how to tell the story. But that's not how you *inform quickly*. The reader, tiring of details and buildup, may not be around when the Big News finally comes.

It's difficult enough to hold a person's attention when you're talking face-to-face — let alone when you're writing. All your reader has to do is glance elsewhere and he or she may be lost forever.

Cure: Tell the Score First

When a reader picks up a report, his or her first concern is with the *bottom line*, or: *What's the most important thing you want me to know/do?* Put another way: *What's the score?*

It's difficult to believe anyone would fail to give the big picture first. Why, then, are so many reports organized *backward*? You may have written reports this way yourself.

Imagine you're assigned to investigate several cases of alleged age discrimination. For each case, you would probably collect all the evidence and then come to some conclusion. Your reasoning would follow an *inductive* pattern: You'd look at specific facts and then proceed to draw a generalization or conclusion about them. If you're not careful, however, you'll *write* your report in the same sequence. You'll give the play-by-play first rather than the score.

Executives don't want diaries. They want writing organized in a *deductive* pattern — conclusions first, followed by the evidence that led to those conclusions.

It's no wonder that, after wading through hundreds of technical reports, the head of a large chemical company issued an edict: "Each report will have a one-page summary of the main conclusions. And don't tell what you did; tell what you found."

Newspaper writing isn't always stellar. Yet, newspapers have at least learned how to dispense important information. In a news story, the first line gives the *bottom line*.

FAULT #3: WRITING LIKE AN INSTITUTION

An editor friendly to a former U.S. president gave him some advice in a newspaper column. He said many of the chief executive's sentences were staid and detached. For instance, the president had told the country:

Tax reductions which go into effect this month have been made financially feasible by substantial reductions in expenditures by government.

The editor suggested a revision emphasizing active, rather than passive, verbs:

We are cutting down your taxes starting this month. We couldn't have done this if we hadn't cut down government expenses.

That's more direct and personal, less institutional. (It still isn't perfect: "Down" isn't needed after "cutting" or "cut.") Another sentence the editor criticized:

The cheapening by inflation of every dollar you earn, every savings account and insurance policy you own, and every pension payment you receive has been halted.

Here the president was doing better because he was talking to each taxpayer in terms of "you." But, again, the editor thought the passage needed more action:

We have stopped the inflation that has cheapened every dollar you earn, every savings account and insurance policy you own, and every pension payment you receive. (Note the shift to "we" and "you" terms.)

Here's the sentence the editor didn't try to translate into plain English:

The proper working relationship between the executive and legislative branches of the federal government has been made more effective. (The president adeptly emphasizes the coequal relationship between branches.)

Cure: Personalize Your Writing

Writers of political speeches err on this point less often than those writing business documents. A politician *must* speak with a personal touch to sway voters.

These same politicians, however, will write memos, letters, and reports in stuffy prose because they feel it's expected of them. They must sound "dignified."

It's a perspective fueled by today's championing of group effort. Many businesspeople no longer speak solely for themselves; they represent a department, a committee, or the entire company. Understandably, they soft-pedal the use of "I." But why neglect "we"? Why write such sentences as:

It will be noted that considerable savings have been accomplished through the initiation of more efficient and effective purchasing procedures.

It sounds as if the achievement was untouched by human hands. Why not recognize both the writer and the reader?

We've saved the company thousands of dollars by improving the way we purchase.

Hardly anybody *speaks* institutional language (unless he or she is *reading* one of those lifeless convention speeches to a bored audience).

When you talk to someone about your business, you speak in terms of "we." Let this natural tendency carry over into your writing as well.

And don't neglect "you." Always consider the other person's point of view. Using plenty of "you's" and "we's" adds warmth and relevance to your writing. The result can be greater and more direct influence over your reader.

Fault #4: Too Much Detail

Take a deep breath and read:

In reviewing bid comparisons for equipment, consideration should be given to the selection of equipment which duplicates that already in service. Sometimes selections of equipment are made with relatively small price differential between the lowest price and that for equipment already installed. Consideration of such comparisons should include the economics of carrying in stock spare parts for a new piece of equipment, as compared to purchasing a duplicate unit. To accomplish this, obtain price quotations for the usual spare parts required for a piece of equipment along with bids for initial cost of the equipment. This spare parts cost represents the initial expense item on a one-time basis and a recurring cost item from the standpoint of taxes and cost of warehousing. It is believed that consideration of the initial cost of spare parts for new equipment and the annual cost of warehousing spare parts is sufficient justification in many cases for the selection of items which duplicate existing equipment.

Do people really write this way? They do. This is an actual example from one of our clients. It has 161 words and a Fog Index[SM] score of 17+.

Now read the writer's own revision. It has 57 words and a Fog Index[SM] score of 10:

When we buy new equipment, sometimes it pays to select items like those already in stock, even if the price is higher. New-type items usually require a new line of spare parts. Their cost to buy and carry may quickly offset any initial price savings on new-type equipment. Keep that in mind when you review equipment bids.

Is anything important left out of the revision?

Cure: Cut With Courage

If you truly understand your subject, you can describe it *simply*, without being *simplistic*. That's the mark of an expert. Only the unsure person burdens you with unnecessary details.

After attending our Clear Writing Seminar, an executive showed us two versions of a bulletin-board announcement. First:

The purpose of this memorandum is to outline a procedure to assure that the oil in the crankcases of the Cushman motor scooters is changed at properly designated intervals.

Cushman scooters are equipped with four-cycle gasoline engines having crankcases that contain oil in the amount of one quart. It is recommended by the manufacturer that the oil in these scooters be changed every 500 miles, but the scooters are not equipped with odometers; therefore, it will be necessary to establish a time interval for oil changes. Inasmuch as it is estimated that the maximum probable mileage is approximately 400 miles per vehicle per month, it has been decided to have the oil changed at that interval.

It will be the responsibility of the operator of each vehicle to see that such vehicle is driven or otherwise transported to the Auto Garage at 30-day intervals for the purpose of obtaining a change of lubricant.

"I took a lot of kidding about this," the executive told us. "Then I remembered the tip you gave us: Before you write, ask yourself: To whom am I writing? And what basically do I want them to know?" Here is his revised announcement:

TO OPERATORS OF CUSHMAN MOTOR SCOOTERS: Please bring your scooters to the Auto Garage every 30 days to have the oil changed.

Fault #5: Important Facts Are Left Out

From a memo sent by a sales representative to the boss:

You asked about that deal with Federated Merchants. It was closed the week after my trip to Chicago. I sold them twice as much as I did on the last trip.

All is fine, provided the sales manager remembers *which* trip to Chicago and how much was sold on the "last trip."

The sales rep is penning a sort of careless *shorthand*.

It happens when the writer presumes what the reader knows and proceeds to omit key facts. Immersed in a project's details, one sometimes loses perspective and expects everyone to know those details as well.

Then there's the type of omission that's simply forgetfulness. Every organization is plagued with the kind of correspondence that asks for a shipment of bolts without mentioning the size or type of thread.

At other times, sheer laziness spurs shorthand. Rather than searching the files to adequately complete the message, the writer takes the easy way out, letting the reader fill in the blanks.

Although a major complaint against business writing is that it's usually too long, no one objects to *necessary* details. There's always room for necessary details if you omit what's unnecessary. The task is to decide which is which.

Cure: Put Yourself in the Reader's Place

When you compose a letter, it's not enough to recall what you want to tell the reader. You must also remember what you *didn't know* about your subject when you knew only as much as your reader.

Whether you're writing a difficult agreement or telling someone how to master a complicated procedure, your description must be clear, concise, complete, and correct.

Put yourself in the reader's place. It's easier to nod agreement to this trusty old piece of advice than to actually follow it. Yet, it can be done — and fairly easily — if you try "resting" your memos, letters, and reports.

The next time you finish a detailed piece of writing, consider it *almost* done. Put it down, walk away, and work on something else for a while. Then return to it. This time, read it as if you're seeing it for the *first* time. Pretend that you know nothing about what's to be presented. In short, pretend you're the reader.

This helps you spot "holes" in your writing — from the little cracks that might only cause your reader to stumble, to the larger ruptures that can level entire understanding.

You can catch obvious flaws by simply reading over your message carefully. The closer you get to your writing, however, the more difficult it becomes to see certain problems. Conversely, the longer your writing "rests" between rewritings, the easier it is to pretend you're the reader. Why? Because in the intervening time you forgot most of the transitions and connective logic that were *in your head* when you first wrote the piece. Without benefit of that additional "text" to help your understanding, you read your writing in much the same way that your audience would.

Fault #6: Pompous Writing

One quick way to change a forthright writer into one who tangles prose is to ask that person to chair a committee.

A committee chairperson can provide the best results by expressing ideas simply. Many forget this timeless truth in the heady contemplation of their new importance. They start to write like bad lawyers.

Here's what one committee chair wrote in announcing a company open house:

The number of persons who will attend any one of the various functions planned for July 4 cannot be reliably estimated until shortly prior to that date. It is therefore desirable that detailed planning be based, and that tentative but noncommitting preparatory measures be initiated, on the assumption that there will be capacity attendance at all functions and that there may be overflows at some.

In other words, planning and prearranging are to be done so that all last-minute adjustments will be downward adjustments, and therefore feasible with minimum difficulty on short notice. This principle will apply especially to such matters as the following, regarding which further word may be issued from time to time as found to be desirable:

The Fog Index[SM] score of that passage is 17+. And the writer used more than twice as many words as needed. If your correspondence isn't getting read, perhaps it, too, suffers from verbal inflation.

Cure: Be Yourself

Dignity begets simplicity. Take Abraham Lincoln, for example. In all history, it would be difficult to find a figure more majestic. He expressed lofty ideas briefly and directly, avoiding the pretentiousness so many business writers embrace.

Of course, one needn't be Lincoln to realize that the announcement on the previous page could be written in simpler words and in half the space:

We can't estimate how many people will attend the functions on July 4 until just before that date. Let's assume all will fill or overflow, but then be prepared to adjust downward on short notice. Keep this in mind as you plan the following:

EXERCISE NO. 1:

Using simpler words and sentence structure, reformat the following passage into a more readable one:

The responsibilities of the Sales Development Division are understood to be: First, to serve in an advisory capacity in screening and evaluation of new products; second, to assist in the selection of those that are the most promising candidates and deemed most likely to prove profitable; third, to initiate, carry out, and coordinate a program for the successful development of each product from the time it is selected as promising until it has reached its maximum profitable sales potential.

(See page 103 for a suggested revision.)

Fault #7: Using Two Words For One

Here's a short sales letter — less than 100 words:

This is to inform you that we have your order dated March 16 for four dozen gold Superior pens, for which we want to express our thanks.

We regret to advise you that we are no longer making this pen in gold and hereby wish to advise that we are currently producing it only in green and black. However, we do have the type you ordered in our Zenith pen. Please advise whether you wish us to ship your order in the Zenith pen.

Awaiting your favorable advice, I remain . . .

Short, yes; but it still uses two words for one. The same message can be halved. When that happens, the odds increase that it will be read, understood, and acted upon.

Here's the same letter, minus the *fog*:

Thank you for your March 16 order for four dozen gold Superior pens.

We now make gold pens only in our Zenith model. Superior pens come in green and black.

May we have your permission to fill your order with Zeniths?

In the second version, 41 words do the work of 90. Further, it avoids distracting language that can derail the reader. And its closing question, unlike the original version's weak ending, invites action.

If you had two letters before you, one twice as long as the other, which would *you* pick up first?

CURE: LEARN TO PLAY "CHOP IT!"

What's more fun than a crossword puzzle and twice as valuable in increasing the power of your writing?

The game is "Chop It!" and the rules are simple: Take any inflated piece of prose and state the same thought in fewer words. The goal is to rid your writing of all useless words. You can play alone or in a group competing for the best score. The Fog Index℠ scale can help gauge your performance.

Rewrite these two paragraphs in half as many words without discarding or changing either paragraph's essence:

EXERCISE NO. 2:

In order to keep you informed of the results of the sales meeting held on June 22 to consider ways and means of reducing the cost of the proposed spring sales campaign, we are submitting herewith a brief résumé and the procedure outlined for the cost-reduction plan.

EXERCISE NO. 3:

Memorandums intended for internal distribution should be written just as carefully as those to be distributed outside the division, and, actually, they serve as an excellent opportunity for developing an individual's proficiency in writing.

Play "Chop It!" at least once a week for 20 minutes, either on your own writing or on someone else's. It's a great way to increase your editing skill.

(You'll find suggested answers to exercises No. 2 and No. 3 on page 104.)

FAULT #8: TOO MANY UNCHECKED COAUTHORS

Fog rarely grows thicker than in the writing done by a "free-range" committee. Each member seeks to leave a mark on the final work. Unchecked changes, though, seldom simplify the message. Rather, they just add more decoration.

The committee-written passage below was the opening page of a manual on report writing. Our guess is that the committee intended to write a "Foreword." But "Forward" may be more appropriate: Some sort of military command is needed to get readers to wade through the *fog*. Nearly one word in three is polysyllabic:

Forward:

The various endeavors of the technical personnel of the Research and Development Department have the common objective of acquiring knowledge and making profitable application of this knowledge within the company's sphere of operations. The mechanics of successfully achieving this objective include the inception of ideas; their experimental trial; the evaluation of experimental results; and, where economically attractive, the adaptation of resultant developments to practice. The medium for the transition of ideas and experimental facts to company decision and action is the recording and reporting system.

The necessity of exercising good practice in the recording of data and reporting of technical information has prompted the preparation of this manual, which is intended to serve both as a guide to new technical employees and as a reminder to more experienced personnel.

Who would — *who could* — read such prose?

CURE: DESIGNATE ONE PERSON AS EDITOR

Committees are formed to solve problems.

Once a committee comes to its conclusions, one person should direct the writing of the report. Members should have an opportunity to review and comment on each other's writing, and certainly they should endorse the report's final version.

But, along the way, as differences of opinion are discussed and resolved, the committee or project leader must supervise the revisions. Cohesive, fluid prose requires a "managing" voice.

One incisive mind (and there were many on the committee mentioned on the previous page) could have steered to a very different "Forward." It might have read:

Foreword:

The Research and Development Department seeks knowledge that can be used profitably. Steps toward this goal include:

- **initiating ideas**
- **testing them experimentally**
- **evaluating results**
- **adopting those that show promise of profit.**

Effective decision making requires all research ideas and data to be carefully recorded and clearly reported.

This manual: (1) guides new technical employees in that process; and (2) reminds others of the process.

Fault #9: Trying to Impress the Boss

The notion that high-level executives prefer to read long-winded prose instead of clear, cogent English is dubious. Busy, "important" people are the last to want their time and patience wasted.

Yet, many remain convinced that writing is judged by the pound. This misconception stems from a desire to impress the boss, coupled with the belief that more is always better. As we've

seen in previous pages, "more" often equals *less understanding*. Hefty writing that confuses the issues and consumes the reader's valuable time makes no sense. So, how *should* you go about dazzling the boss?

Your writing will impress people if you can locate and summarize the key ideas from the mass of detail.

You might argue, "I spent weeks researching my subject. If I can sum it up in a couple of pages, will all I've done be appreciated?" If your boss is like most executives we know, he or she will stand up and cheer at finding someone (you!) who understands the burden of a busy person's reading time.

If you feel compelled to explain your brevity, consider prefacing your report with something like this:

This research took several weeks. Much information was collected, cataloged, and synthesized. More importantly, we learned enough about the subject to find the basic causes of the problem. Here are our findings, which we have carefully pared into a concise — *but complete* — report.

CURE: REMEMBER THAT THE BOSS IS HUMAN

Suppose you have a sharp boss, one of the brightest in the company. Does that mean that he or she *likes* to muddle through hard reading? Such people *can* find their way past challenging articles on taxes, finance, or law. And they're willing to do so when there's no other way to get the information.

But what does the same executive read during leisure time? Some may subscribe to *Harper's* or *Atlantic*. These magazines often discuss complex issues but, as we have shown, their words and sentences are simpler than most business writing. The authors are highly skilled at knowing how to write clearly without exhausting the reader.

This is true of most professional writers. In fact, you might define a good writer as one who

- has something to say

- says it completely and correctly, but also clearly and concisely

- exhibits such grace that the work seems effortless.

Even if your boss holds a Ph.D., you'll be thanked for writing as simply — and as thoroughly — as you can. You'll save his or her time, effort, and patience.

What about those who seldom read heavier material than, say, *Reader's Digest*? Again, they *can* read much tougher material *if* they have to. You can bet that if someone left them a million dollars, with the stipulations written in Sanskrit, they'd find a way to decipher the message. But no business executive *seeks* hard reading. Help your boss by simplifying your writing. Do this by keeping your Fog Index℠ score generally below 12.

FAULT #10: WEAK BEGINNINGS AND ENDINGS

Most business writers have shed old-fashioned forms of letter writing. Opening paragraphs like this are now less likely to appear in your morning mail:

Your communication of June 9 has come to our attention and has been duly noted by all concerned. Pursuant to the same, we are pleased to herein report . . .

Still, many business writers "tighten up" and become very formal when they begin letters. Several we analyzed began something like this:

This is to acknowledge and thank you for your letter of June 9. . . .; or: Reference is hereby made to your memorandum of June 9. . . .

Usually, it's important to mention the date of the other person's letter. But why say you've received it? Isn't that obvious? Why not get right to the point?

On June 9, you asked if we produce . . .

Or, if a more courteous beginning is desired:

Thank you for your June 9 letter. . . .

Many business writers will also slip on courtesy "closes." They may have outgrown such mildewed expressions as "We beg to remain," but they don't distinguish between courtesy and palaver. They write, "We should be deeply grateful for the favor of a reply from you at your earliest convenience," when "We hope to hear from you soon" would say as much.

CURE: PICTURE YOUR READER LISTENING INSTEAD OF READING

One characteristic of well-written prose is that you can almost hear the writer speaking.

That should be your guide as you begin any business correspondence. Picture your reader and ask yourself: *What would I say if the person were on the phone or across my desk?*

This practice will keep you from producing flowery phrases that sound stuffy. Let the way you'd speak (excepting your slang, repetition, and incomplete thoughts!) guide your writing. You'll then avoid such absurdities as:

Dear Darla Rae:

In accordance with suggestions embodied in your memorandum of February 22, issuance of a supplement to the April report was hence undertaken. Two (2) copies of the aforementioned supplement are enclosed herewith for your information and records. We beg to express our gratitude for your thoughtful suggestion and hope that you give forthcoming reports the same kind of carefully conceived consideration.

Can you imagine actually *saying* those words to "Dear Darla Rae" if you met face-to-face? More likely, you'd just say:

On February 22, you suggested we issue a supplement to the April report. Here are two copies of it. Thanks for your thoughtful suggestions. Keep them coming.

You can't always write the way *you* speak. Some subjects and some audiences mandate a different approach. Whatever your style, however, listen to how it sounds.

FAULT #11: USING LONG WORDS UNNECESSARILY

Here's a rather simple idea made obtuse:

In our endeavor to ascertain whether the proposals we have formulated are fundamentally sound, we anticipate engaging the services of a market research organization to determine whether our conceptualization of the market can be substantiated by information accumulated in the field.

The writer uses language no one speaks and few would want to read. Note the unnecessary use of long words, a common fault of business writers. In the revision below, the writer has found simpler substitutes for a dozen words without any loss in overall meaning:

To learn if our plans are sound, we expect to hire a market research firm to check our market view against field-gathered facts.

Longer synonyms are sometimes needed to avoid tiresome repetition. Frequently, we hear business writers tell us they use words like "endeavor," "terminate," and "utilization" only in relief of "try," "end," and "use." But a look at their writing reveals that they first use the longer words repeatedly *before* using the shorter ones.

Long words are fine, *if* they're needed. Save them for times when only they have the precise meanings needed to express your ideas. Otherwise, let short, familiar words carry the burden of your thought. In that way, your writing will be easier to read, and you'll still have room for your *necessary* long words.

CURE: CHOOSE THE SHORT WORD

Here are some words commonly overworked in business writing. Next to each provide a shorter, simpler word that will serve often (not always) as a good substitute. (Some of the words have more than one meaning, allowing for more than one answer.)

Accumulate _____	Initial _____
Additional _____	Initiate _____
Aggregate _____	Locality _____
Ameliorate _____	Maintenance _____
Anticipate _____	Materialize _____
Approximately _____	Modification _____
Assistance _____	Notwithstanding _____
Commence _____	Objective _____
Commitment _____	Optimum_____
Compensate _____	Preparatory_____
Component _____	Proceed _____
Construct _____	Procure_____
Demonstrate _____	Proficiency_____
Distribute _____	Purchase _____
Downsize _____	Reimburse _____
Encounter _____	Subsequent _____
Endeavor _____	Substantiate_____
Equivalent _____	Sufficient _____
Explicit _____	Terminate_____
Fundamental _____	Transmit_____
Inasmuch _____	Utilization _____

(Check your answers against those on the next page.)

PREFER THE SHORT WORD

Accumulate ....gather

Additional ....more

Aggregate.............total

Ameliorate...........improve

Anticipate.............expect

Approximately.....about

Assistance.............help

Commence ....begin

Commitment........promise

Compensate ....pay

Component..........part

Construct.............build

Initial ....first

Initiate.........................begin

Locality ....place

Maintenance..............upkeep

Materialize.................develop

Modification ....change

Notwithstanding.......despite

Objective ....goal

Optimum ....best

Preparatory...............planned

Proceed ....start

Procure.......................get

Demonstrate	show	Proficiency	skill
Distribute	give	Purchase	buy
Downsize	cut	Reimburse	repay
Encounter	meet	Subsequent	next
Endeavor	try	Substantiate	prove
Equivalent	equal	Sufficient	enough
Explicit	clear	Terminate	end
Fundamental	basic	Transmit	send
Inasmuch	given	Utilization	use

We emphasize that there's nothing wrong with using a long word when no other choice will quite do. Unfortunately, long words are usually chosen only because *they are long*. If you can't justify using a long word, opt for its shorter version.

SAMPLES: THE LONG AND SHORT WAY

44 WORDS

It is the responsibility of the head of each and every department to properly arrange and coordinate his or her affairs in such a manner that all salaried employees, including the manager, will receive the full vacation period to which they are rightfully entitled.

13 WORDS

Each department head must ensure that all salaried employees get a full vacation.

37 WORDS

Careful thought and deliberation should be given to any benefits accruing to the company from your attendance at any convention or meeting before your submission of a request for a travel-expense voucher for such a trip.

19 WORDS

Before you ask for money to attend a convention or meeting, be sure the event will benefit the company.

46 WORDS

Reference to our payment ledger indicates that the January account in the amount of $425 is outstanding. Please send us your remittance at your earliest convenience. If you require an additional notice, please let us know so that a duplicate can be forwarded by return mail.

18 WORDS

We would greatly appreciate receiving the $425 owed us since January. A copy of the bill is enclosed.

29 WORDS

It is hoped that the parents of the children attending the Macon School will insist that the children keep all of the appointments that will be given to them.

16 WORDS

We hope that parents of Macon School children will insist that their children keep all appointments.

FAULT #12: FAILURE TO REVISE

Polished prose doesn't just happen. Good writers revise and revise . . . and then revise some more. They know they can't just dash off their ideas and expect everyone to understand them automatically.

Perhaps, similarly, if the writers of these headlines had been more careful, they wouldn't have penned two of our all-time favorites:

Man Killed by Bear Identified as Cuban

(*Las Vegas Review Journal*, September 28, 1982)

LDS Head Has Surgery for Blood Clots on Brain

(*Santa Barbara News-Press*, September 20, 1990)

Often, the first draft of any memo, letter, or report is littered with verbal debris. Because you're focusing on the *thought* you want to develop, you tend to neglect the nuances of your word choices.

To eliminate confusing and embarrassing constructions, always reread what you have written — especially if someone else has typed it. Too many foolish and costly mistakes happen when you don't. If time allows, fine-tune your writing, adding what is needed, and cutting what is not.

Granted, those who write a lot won't have time — and shouldn't take time — to redraft every paper.

Unless the product is especially faulty, let it go. But sometime during the week, take 20 minutes or so to read over some of your previous work. Begin by critiquing each sentence, then move to each paragraph. By doing this, you'll learn how to spot — and avoid — bad habits.

Cure: Become Your Own Critic

No one leaves school a finished writer. You must continue your training by learning how to teach *yourself*. Become your toughest, most discerning critic. When drafting and editing your prose, remember the Writer's Golden Rule: *Write unto others as you want others to write unto you.*

Count how many trite, useless words can be cut from this passage:

We wish to advise you that we have thoroughly and completely reviewed our July transactions with you and accordingly are attaching for your information a transcript of your account as it appears in our records. With respect to your claim for $1.50 a gallon allowance, we wish to advise you that it has been granted. Enclosed is our check in the amount of $150.

"Wish to advise," "accordingly," and "for your information" add nothing to the message. Another unneeded phrase commonly used, "in the amount of," is easily replaced by "for." Moreover, why not start with the good news: "Enclosed is our check for $150"?

EXERCISE NO. 4:

Delete the unnecessary words in this passage:

The Committee recommends that the cost of dinners be excluded from the amount considered for tuition refunds. This will reduce the amount of refund from $560 under the present policy to $455 under the new policy if the tuition is paid in cash, or from $630 under the present policy to $518 under the new policy if the tuition is paid in installments. This change will bring our application of the Refund Plan into close agreement with the practice of other companies.

(See page 104 for a suggested revision.)

FAULT #13: PASSIVE WRITING

In active voice, a sentence's subject commits the action: "I [subject] bought [active verb] a new computer." In passive voice, a subject is *acted on*: "A new computer [subject] was bought [passive verb] by me."

Active voice pervades our speech, whether in regard to sports, politics, or business. When people talk to one another, it's natural to start with themselves (the actor): "I think . . . ," not "It is thought by me . . ."

Similarly, an executive will *tell* another, "We found we lost money by owning our warehouses instead of leasing them." But then he or she will *write*:

It was found that money was lost through the ownership of company warehouses, and that a program to lease them was preferable.

Such stilted, *foggy* language hampers easy reading. It also lacks punch because it leads with a "to be" verb form (was), rather than an action form ("found").

Some claim that the passive voice enables business writing to remain objective and impersonal by de-emphasizing the actor/writer. More often, the writer *wants* to straddle the issue and escape responsibility for what's written. The actor is pluralized and then relegated to a prepositional phrase ("It was found *by us* . . ."). Or worse, the "by us" is dropped altogether, and *who* did the finding becomes a mystery.

Finally, many passive voice uses are downright silly. A playful professor of business communication we know offers her students this tongue-in-cheek example: "It is thought by me that Hell should be gone to by you."

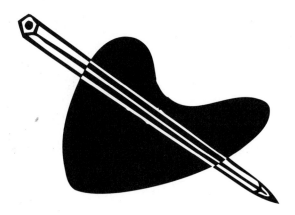

CURE: USE ACTIVE VERBS

Passive voice *does* have its uses. Sometimes the object *acted on* needs to be emphasized more than the actor:

The crucial documents were destroyed. The VP of Quality Control was fired. The likable corporate attorney was picked for the job.

Make it a practice, however, to prefer more natural, active verbs in your writing. Your sentences will be clearer, shorter, and sharper. Here are some comparisons:

PASSIVE

It has been revealed by experience that the public relations campaign is requiring more time than had been anticipated.

It has been learned that a return to our former procedure can be made without loss.

Our sales plans are predicated on the assumption that increased buying will be engaged in by the public this spring.

An improvement in quality was made.

When an application of wax is made to the table's surface, a brilliance is imparted to it.

ACTIVE

Experience reveals that the public relations campaign requires more time than we anticipated.

We now know we can return to our former procedure without loss.

Our sales plans assume that the public will buy more this spring.

Quality improved.

Waxing will brighten the table's surface.

Fault #14: Smothered Verbs

Let's talk more about verbs.

The verb can be the strongest word in a sentence, or the weakest. Used keenly, verbs invigorate writing. Misused, they create *fog*.

Overuse of passive voice, as seen previously, is one potential problem. Another is the weakening of verbs by turning them into nouns. Noun endings that alert you to smothered verbs include *-ion, -tion, -ing, -ment, -ant, -ent, -ance,* and *-able.*

Compare the press release at the left to the newspaper story at the right:

Smothered Verbs

Allen Jones, secretary, called public atten*tion* Friday to resump*tion* of operations by the State Tax League. The deci*sion* in favor of incorpora*tion* was noted in the announce*ment*. Enroll*ment* of members will be encouraged by elimina*tion* of individual financial responsibility, which is the resul*tant* of incorpora*tion*.

Active Verbs

The State Tax League is operating again, Secretary Allen Jones announced Friday. The League decided to incorporate, he said. More members are expected to enroll because the move frees them of personal financial responsibility.

Take another example. If you're telling a friend about a baseball game, you might say:

Slugger *hit* a low drive. Stretch *grabbed* it and *fired* it to first for the putout.

In "professional" business prose, full of smothered verbs, the report would go like this:

The *hitting* of a low drive *was accomplished* by Slugger. *Interception* of the ball *was effected* by Stretch, and the *motivation* of it to first for the putout *was executed* by the same member of the team.

CURE: REFRAIN FROM "NOUNIZING" VERBS

Instead of writing, "We'll substitute No. 4s for No. 5s," the smotherer states, "We'll *make* substitu*tion* of No. 4s for No. 5s."

The habit quickly mushrooms. The smotherer transforms every simple active verb into swollen, stagy phrasing:

acquire becomes *seek acquisition*

adjust . . . *create an adjustment*

alter . . . *make alteration*

assist . . . *render assistance*

conclude . . . *come to a conclusion*

decide . . . *arrive at a decision*

discuss . . . *engage in a discussion*

estimate . . . *offer an estimation*

evaluate . . . *perform an evaluation*

indicate . . . *give indication*

locate . . . *ascertain the location*

study . . . *do a study*

undertake . . . *venture an undertaking*

Exercise No. 5:

Rewrite this paragraph, restoring action to passive and smothered verbs:

In a letter dated August 17, information was requested by you concerning measurement methods being followed in connection with deliveries of our bulk products. Discussion of this was engaged in several years ago. Report No. 334 covering the subject having been issued September 27, 1982. Methods now being followed are substantially similar to those that were in effect at that time.

(See page 104 for the authors' suggested revision.)

FAULT #15: VAGUE, ABSTRACT WORDS

To write compellingly, learn to use concrete, specific terms instead of vague, abstract ones.

A sales manager writing a pamphlet to describe the features of a point-of-sale display begins:

This unit is designed for maximum flexibility and adaptability. Practically every retailer, large or small, can use this display advantageously.

Exactly what does that tell a prospective buyer? "Flexibility," "adaptability," and "advantageously" are abstractions. They don't denote specific functions or actions. They don't grab the reader's attention.

When we asked the sales manager what she meant, her talk became spirited, animated . . . concretized:

There are five backgrounds to the display. You can use one by itself, or two or three together. You can set them up in a straight line, or at any angle. (So *that's* what she meant by "flexibility.") She continued:

In a small store, you can make a continuous display along a wall. If you have a large store, you can place several displays on the selling floor. (*Now* she's defining "adaptability.")

These displays cause customers to stop and look at the product. They explain the product, enhance interest, and increase sales. (*Finally,* she's specifying what "advantageously" is.)

CURE: USE CONCRETE WORDS

The original paragraph appeared in a suggestion box. The revision was drafted after the writer was interviewed by her supervisor, who advised using more concrete terms:

ORIGINAL

In order to gain optimum utilization of the by-products of our refining activities and simultaneously achieve economic advantages from our selling activities in the textile industry, it is recommended that we convert DXN into RLM, which could be utilized as a sizing solution for woven materials.

REVISION

Each day we produce 20 barrels of DXN, a by-product for which we have no present use. Meanwhile, our sales force sells only four products to textile makers.

The DXN could be economically converted into RLM for use as sizing for cloth. We would then profit from a substance now wasted. And our sales force would have another product to offer the textile trade.

The original version reflected a good idea, but one masked by vague, abstract words. "Optimum utilization," "activities," and "economic advantages" don't summon rich, vivid images to mind.

Once the writer became aware of her language, she substituted more vivid, concrete choices. Her revised suggestion was adopted by the company.

You'll produce a vibrant message that beckons your reader if you use words that stand for things you can touch and operations you can demonstrate.

FAULT #16: RUNAWAY SENTENCES

Writing that ignores the period and shuns the single-thought sentence becomes an uninviting, solid block of type. The fault is most prevalent among those who dictate.

In his book *On Writing Well*, William Zinsser says, "If you find yourself hopelessly mired in a long sentence, it's probably because you are trying to make the sentence do more than it can reasonably do — perhaps express two dissimilar thoughts." Here's a classic example:

Assuming the material to be converted in the Apex Company 100-gallon mixer in their plant and in its present operating condition (three batches per hour, stopping the machine five minutes to empty and refill), and with the condition of shipping the material from Apex to Acme packing in

one-quart containers, reshipping to Apex for labeling and the hand-packing of 12 cans per carton, including allowance for waste, trucking, etc., the cost would be $2.432 per carton of 12 one-quart cans.

That's what we call a runaway sentence. The writer's thoughts gallop along unharnessed.

Use periods to separate — and thus emphasize — main ideas. When this is done to the paragraph above, we get:

Let's assume the following: (1) The material would be converted in the Apex Company's 100-gallon mixer. It now turns out three batches an hour, stopping five minutes for each refill. (2) Apex will ship the material to Acme, where it will be packed in one-quart containers. (3) Acme will ship it back to Apex for labeling and hand-packing, 12 cans to a carton. If we allow for waste, delay, and trucking, the cost would be $2.432 per carton of 12 one-quart cans.

es running sentences

CURE: PREWRITE YOUR MESSAGE

The ability to write a "passable" first draft can save time and effort. You can develop this skill by preparing and corralling your thoughts *before* you write. This will prevent your sentences from running away.

Try composing a brief outline listing all your main and supporting points. Put them into short, concise *sentences* — not phrases or single words. This forces you to think precisely and to capture the essence (or action) of your points.

Or, you might do all this mentally. Some writers can compose, organize, and redraft in their heads. They see and correct flaws before ever touching a pen, recorder, or keyboard.

Whatever method you choose, you'll be *prewriting* your message.

running sentences

Try stopping this runaway sentence. Substitute periods for connectives and redraft its structure:

To help eliminate any possible misunderstanding during your test runs in the tower, which might result in an unsatisfactory product from the drier (such as one with impurities), I would like to know what you would think of your people printing an advance run-sheet on which such information as when the run is to take place, which cycles can be dried with accelerated rates through the drier, which cycles are to be good cycles requiring a clean tower and a slow rate, etc., can be summarized.

Fault #17: Weak Vocabulary

The largest English dictionaries contain about 650,000 words. Some businesspeople, particularly those at the top, have impressive vocabularies. (Perhaps you've seen surveys linking executive ability and vocabulary size.) Still, those knowing many words command only about 30,000. Fifty-thousand would be tops, even for the most learned.

Clearly, most of us understand only a fraction of our language. For the average businessperson, that means 18,000-25,000 words.

While this book applauds simple writing, it doesn't advise having a simple vocabulary. You can't ignore your vocabulary and hope to gain control of language.

A bigger, better vocabulary helps in four ways:

1. Some of the longer words you'll know will be briefer and more precise than their substitutes (for example, "modification" vs. "a slight change").

2. A large vocabulary gives you many more *short*, forceful words from which to choose.

3. Words are tools not just for reading and writing, but for *thinking*. Related concepts are richly combined and better understood by such words as "thermodynamics" for the engineer, "perspective" for the artist or critic, and "schizophrenic" for the psychologist.

4. Communication is a two-way process: If your vocabulary is limited, you may not understand others.

CURE: INCREASE YOUR WORD CONTROL

A skilled writer or speaker knows how to string even simple, everyday words in clever, imaginative ways.

In *Semantics*, Hugh Walpole's helpful book about words and their meanings, he chides those who emphasize only the need to learn new words:

If we cannot make friends and become high executives, and if we blame our failure upon our poor mastery of words, our plight is not due to the smallness of our vocabulary. Miracles can be worked with a couple of thousand words. . . . We are weak not because our vocabulary is inadequate, but because we are stale in the way we use it.

That statement might well be framed and hung in every business office.

Few have better illustrated Walpole's point than Franklin D. Roosevelt when he told a nation ravaged by economic depression:

The only thing we have to fear is fear itself.

Later, John F. Kennedy would say in his inaugural address:

Let every nation know, whether it wishes us well or ill, that we shall pay any price, bear any burden, meet any hardship, support any friend, oppose any foe to assure the survival and the success of liberty.

Such statements gain force from common words used in fresh ways.

To achieve this skill, even on a small scale, you must master more words. You have thousands in your reading vocabulary that you don't express, either because you're uncertain of their meanings, or uncomfortable with their use. Once you become closely acquainted with even the simplest word, you'll find its meaning — and potential use — much broader than expected.

FAULT #18: GROSS GRAMMAR

Do the following sentences contain errors in grammar?

1. **When he inquired over the telephone, I replied, "It is me."**   ( ) YES   ( ) No

2. **Can I borrow your laptop computer for the weekend?**   ( ) YES   ( ) No

3. **Has everyone turned in their report?**   ( ) YES   ( ) No

4. **She did really good on the exam.**   ( ) YES   ( ) No

5. **He should have went to the study session.**   ( ) YES   ( ) No

If you replied YES to each question, you're right. The statements should read: (1) It is *I*; (2) *May* I borrow . . . ; (3) . . . turned in *his* (or *her*) . . . ; (4) She did really *well* . . . ; and (5) He should have *gone* . . .

These mistakes are common — so common, in fact, that many readers won't detect them. You might then ask, "So why worry about grammar?"

The answer is simple: Grammatical errors can *interfere with communication*, and they can *swiftly lower your credibility*.

Gross mistakes will confuse your reader:

Police observed a man chasing a cat with a broom in his pajamas.

Moreover, how do such sentences affect the audience's sense of *you*? Are they apt to see a bright, educated person who thinks and writes with care?

Cure: See the Larger Picture

It would be fine if every reader of this book became an enthusiastic student of grammar. However, that's neither likely nor necessary.

Effective business writers needn't memorize every rule of grammar, punctuation, or usage, but they must know enough not to write: "He don't..."; "They was..."; or "We ain't got...."

Most business writers have developed far beyond such barbarisms. Just about anyone who has major writing responsibilities knows the basics of good grammar.

Rather, business writers worry about split infinitives and sentence-ending prepositions. They fret over minor details, all the while ignoring the more crucial issue of whether they're communicating effectively. They lose sight of what's really important.

To those who freeze when they approach a writing job for fear they'll commit grammatical errors, our advice is simple: Relax. In 50 years of surveying business writing, we've found that *fog* — not grammar — underlies most poor writing.

A simple way to help ensure good grammar is to follow these two steps:

1. Write what you have to say as simply and directly as possible.

2. Examine what you have written to make sure the reader can't easily misinterpret your message.

It may comfort you to know that William Shakespeare labored along without benefit of schooling in grammar. The first printed English grammar book didn't appear until about a century after he wrote his plays.

Fault #19: Lack of Variety

Occasionally, someone tells us, "If business writers follow your ideas, they'll all write alike."

How ironic! If ever a place existed where all prose sounds the same, it's the world of business. Nearly everyone has the same *deadly* style — bankers, accountants, lawyers, engineers, technicians . . . The jargon may differ, but the style remains just as bleak. Somehow, it's equated with propriety and professionalism.

Indeed, no writing suffers more from sameness than American business English. Every message seems monotonous. You can't tell Nelson's writing from Witowski's, nor Murphy's from Minetti's. The human juice is squeezed out. What's left is a lifeless writing far less potent than possible.

When you do receive a message that mirrors a living person, it's a welcome sight. You're apt to pay attention and heed the content. What's more, you can count on this: Anytime you find such a message, it'll have a low Fog Index^{SM} score. Simplicity and vitality go hand in hand.

Standardization is unavoidable in large organizations. Routine work must be guided by established procedures; they make mass production possible. Sameness, though, has its dangers — especially when it comes to communication.

Cure: Find Your Voice

Here's another test of good prose: Can your audience almost "hear" you as they read your writing?

Projecting a distinct, recognizable voice is harder than it looks. You must know who you are, what you want, and who and what you hope to become. In short, you must know yourself.

Most *fogged* writing in business (and other organizations) is produced by those unsure of themselves. They retreat from any conviction by writing in the inert style of the bureaucrat. And they try to show they *belong* by adopting the jargon of some limited group.

To advance in any field, you must have a clear sense of identity and purpose. These qualities inform the substance and style of your writing.

Those fearing that simplicity leads to sameness should observe the professional writing field. Nearly all best-selling books, successful plays, popular magazine articles, and syndicated newspaper columns average a Fog Index[SM] score no higher than 12. But, we also find the most stylistic variety among the authors of these works. Why? Because no two people are alike. No one communicates exactly the same as someone else.

When you come to know and accept yourself, *your* literary voice will emerge.

Fault #20: Poor Organization

A frequent complaint of business writing is that it's poorly organized. So many faults are bundled in this criticism that it's one of the hardest to correct.

Clear organization is the result of clear thought, and you can't think clearly about a problem unless you have a good understanding of it, coupled with the intelligence to reach logical conclusions.

Clear thought allows you to highlight crucial ideas, subordinate what's less important, and forgo unneeded detail.

It's helpful to think of an *informative* business message as if it were a conversation. Tell your reader, right from the start, *what* you're describing and *why*. Proceed to summarize your conclusions. Then go back and describe them in detail, beginning with the first. Be certain to cover how you got your information and how it supports your descriptive summaries.

Similarly, most *persuasive* business messages begin with the "bottom line," i.e., the writer's main purpose. For example:

Tony should not be our CEO.

Purpose statements are supported by *main points* or reasons why:

- He's dishonest
- He's incompetent
- He's emotionally unstable.

Each of these three main points may be further developed by subpoints. Subpoints make any organization easier to follow by showing how ideas relate:

He's dishonest because he (a) lies, (b) distorts, (c) cheats, and (d) steals.

No doubt he doesn't write well either.

Cure: Outline Before You Write

To make sense of anything you write, your audience expends energy. First, the reader must "recognize" your words. Then *their arrangement* must be processed into ideas. These ideas must be further processed into relationships.

Recall how you act as a reader. Say you get two letters in the same mail. One is a solid block of single-spaced, uniform type. The other is formatted into several paragraphs with (1) headings and subheadings; (2) numbered and bulleted points; and (3) underlined, italicized, and boldfaced text. Which would you pick up first?

Most of us would choose the letter with attractive design. Experience tells us it's probably better organized because the writer cared about clarifying ideas.

Good writing requires thought and effort. Or, as Blaise Pascal explained, "I have made this [letter] longer than usual, only because I have not had the time to make it shorter." When you *do* take the time, you'll rid your writing of *fog*-causing problems. You'll lessen your reader's work.

Realize that the outline is the skeleton of your message. It should shape your writing in a way that enhances readability. So before you write, *outline*. Jot down the main points you want to make. Under each, sequence the subpoints and evidence you'll use for support. Then go back and arrange your main points.

Some skilled writers, as noted earlier, can outline in their heads. However, no one can write clearly without first having some plan. Spilling information without an outline is like dropping bricks from a truck and expecting a wall to fall in place.

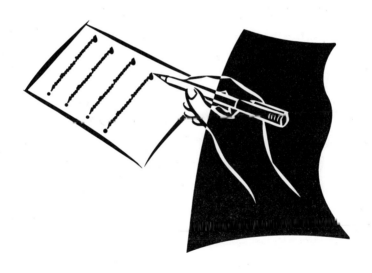

FAULT #21: HEDGING

The double and triple hedge weakens business writing. From the overly cautious will come:

It *appears* that *perhaps it may* be possible to fill your order by the 28th of the month.

Three hedging words — "appears," "perhaps," and "may" — in a single sentence? Any *one* would have communicated the necessary qualification. By overqualifying, the writer appears unsure and unreliable.

Write as strongly as the facts allow. If you must qualify, do so; your words shouldn't mislead. But resist the habit of *overusing* "appears," "perhaps," "may," "might," "seems," "possibly," "generally," "usually," "apparently," and "approximately."

If you must qualify, build trust by doing it directly:

Barring the possibility of a work stoppage here, we'll ship your order by June 28.

And if you make a mistake, admit it. Not like this:

Apparently, according to our records, your payment was received somewhat late last month. Accordingly, you may choose to disregard our last letter.

A letter free of hedging helps maintain your credibility:

We *do* have your payment. Our last letter was a mistake and must have concerned you. Please forgive us for sending it.

CURE: WRITE WITH CONFIDENCE

Lack of confidence leads to *fog*. Clear writing comes from knowing what to say and then saying it simply and directly.

This doesn't mean you'll always have all the facts, or that you can trust all the ones you do have. Still, you should know which facts you're certain of and which ones you're not. The reader deserves no less.

Writers hedge to protect themselves. They believe that hedging insulates against criticism and blame. But who is seen as weak and vulnerable: the person who forever qualifies, or the one unafraid to state the facts and the limits of his or her knowledge? Put another way, what judgments would you make about these two authors?

HEDGER

In reply to your inquiry it should be said that generally our No. 4 fuel has appeared to be associated with the best performance in the FG engine, which apparently it seems is the one you have in operation from the description you have given us. It is our considered opinion that quite possibly that fuel, or perhaps our No. 5 if the weather is approaching the cold side, should possibly give the most satisfactory results.

SIMPLIFIER

From your description, we believe you have an FG engine. If so, we recommend our No. 4 fuel for the best performance. Some customers report that in cold weather they prefer our No. 5 fuel. You may wish to try it as well.

By confronting the customer's problem, the Simplifier reflects and instills confidence.

FAULT #22: ROUNDABOUT PHRASES

Nothing mutes the impact of your message more than wasted space. In writing, every word counts.

Roundabout phrases flourish in business writing, where somehow they're seen as "thoughtful," "appropriate" posture. So pervasive is their use that we seldom stop to consider what they mean. When we do, we realize that they say little or nothing.

Take the variations of this all-too-familiar opening:

We would like to talk with you . . .

concerning the matter of . . .

in connection with . . .

in relation to . . .

on the subject of . . .

relative to the issue of . . .

with reference to . . .

with regard to . . .

with respect to . . .

. . . our new line of merchandise.

One word — "about" — could replace any prepositional phrase above. The result would be a tighter, smoother sentence.

Why, for example, would so many people say, "We are in receipt of . . ."? Does it mean any more than "We received . . ."?

And how many times have you seen accountants write, "A check in the amount of $50 . . ."? "In the amount of . . ." sometimes will appear half a dozen times in one letter. What does it mean, other than "for"? Why not: "A check for $50 . . ."? Or: "A $50 check . . ."?

CURE: CHOOSE DIRECT ROUTES

Sensitize yourself to habit phrases that detour your prose and squander your reader's time.

Below are several popular roundabouts. Next to each, provide a shorter "direct route":

at an early date _____

at the present time _____

at this point in time _____

despite the fact that _____

due to the fact that _____

during the time that _____

enclosed herewith _____

for the purpose of _____

for the reason that _____

goes under the name of _____

in behalf of _____

in large measure _____

in order that _____

in order to _____

in recognition of this fact _____

in the course of _____

in the event that _____

in the near future _____

in the vicinity of _____

it is often the case that _____

notwithstanding the fact that _____

on a few occasions _____

on a regular basis _____

performs the function of _____

provided that _____

serves the function of being _____

under the circumstances _____

until such time _____

we are of the opinion _____

(Check your answers against those on page 94.)

DIRECT ROUTES

at an early date	soon
at the present time	now
at this point in time	now
despite the fact that	although
due to the fact that	because
during the time that	during
enclosed herewith	enclosed
for the purpose of	for, to
for the reason that	because
goes under the name of	is called
in behalf of	for
in large measure	largely
in order that	for, so
in order to	to
in recognition of this fact	consequently
in the course of	during
in the event that	if
in the near future	soon
in the vicinity of	near
it is often the case that	often
notwithstanding the fact that	although
on a few occasions	occasionally
on a regular basis	regularly

performs the function of ....functions

provided that ....if

serves the function of being ....is

under the circumstances ....given, because

until such time ....until

we are of the opinion..............................we think

Rounding Up More Roundabouts ...

a large number of...many

a number of ....some, several

all over the world...worldwide

are in need of..need

as a matter of fact..in fact

as a means of informing ....to inform

as of late ....lately

by means of ....with, by

continue to be able to ....continue to

eliminate the occurrence of ....eliminate

finish the completion of ....finish, complete

for the purpose of examining...........................to examine

in a situation in which ....when

in a state of change ....changing

in light of the fact that......................................because, given

in the field of ....in

is based on the assumption ....assumes

is based on the inference...................................infers

is responsible for choosing ....chooses

it is probable that ....probably

it would seem that..apparently

make it possible..enable make provisions for..provide

most of the time ....usually

negate the possibility of....................................preclude

prior to the start of ....before

read through..read

take the place of...replace

the early part of next week................................early next week

the issue at hand ....the issue

the issue in question...the issue

there is little doubt..probably

there is some doubt ....possibly

FAULT #23: FALSE COURTESY

Courtesy and friendliness must be genuine. When they routinely appear only out of obligation, anyone can tell they're phony.

Openings and closings of letters are good examples. Isn't it silly to call some stranger, or even some customer, "Dear"? "Dear Mr. Neal . . ." Then you tell him at the end that you're "truly" his.

Most of us keep using these phrases. "They're just gestures — no one takes them literally," we say.

Many companies, however, have modernized their letters to eliminate such phrases. They write the recipient's name and address at the top of the page, beginning at the left margin. Then they skip a line or two and launch into the body of the letter. At the end of the message, they type the name and perhaps the title of the sender, who signs above.

Warmth and friendliness are conveyed by tone, rather than by such worn phrases as "sincerely yours," "yours truly," and "respectfully yours."

Even if company policy doesn't free you to take this step, you can avoid other useless words that convey hollow courtesy. Here's how:

FAWNING

We eagerly wish to solicit any recommendations you may want to make, and we hope to assure you that such valued suggestions will receive our careful and immediate consideration.

CONVINCING

Please give us your suggestions. We'll consider them carefully.

CURE: CARE ABOUT YOUR READER

If you truly want to serve your reader, show it. Reply promptly, answer the questions asked, and make it clear that you're eager to help. Actions speak louder than words.

If you've given the information or help requested, you won't need the sort of final paragraph that seems so rote:

We sincerely hope this is the information you desire. Please feel free to let us know if we can answer any additional questions or be of any further assistance.

Instead, you might say:

If you need more information, let us know.

Sometimes, a letter will come across as too blunt. In an effort to be concise, or lacking interest in the reader, the writer appears abrupt, if not abrasive. Take the example of a salesperson for a steel-fabricating company who replied to a letter asking for quotations on steel swimming pools:

We don't make steel swimming pools and we don't intend to.

Had the writer cared about the reader, he could have been courteous as well as brief:

I'm sorry, but we don't make steel swimming pools. We suggest you contact a fabricator in your city. The ABC Company, for example, should be able to help you.

Because some people load their business letters with hackneyed phrases, they feel a letter of only a line or two is rude. However, we've never met a person who resented receiving a short letter that was friendly and complete.

FAULT #24: POOR EDITING BY SUPERVISORS

Supervisors hold their jobs because of some specialized, work-related knowledge. Yet, because they supervise others, they're also expected to be *editors*.

In the professional writing field, no one becomes an editor without extensive writing experience, along with skill in helping other writers.

But, in many large businesses today, the writing of every departmental person goes out over the supervisor's signature. It's natural for him or her to want a hand in how staffers write. (Even if the supervisor doesn't sign all the letters, he or she is responsible for their content.)

Trouble may arise when he or she tries to tell others how to write. Frequently, the supervisor knows something is wrong with the writing, but can't quite figure out what it is or how to correct it. If he or she gives the wrong remedy, the product may worsen. On the other hand, providing no guidance leaves the staffer confused and frustrated.

So, before you complain about the supervisor's changes to your writing, realize that editing is a tough job — and one for which your supervisor probably lacks formal training.

Even in the professional writing field, writers and editors wage war. Writers see editors' changes as trivial or stupid. Editors complain that writers fail in their grammar and logic. Yet, together, they work out their differences and improve the final product.

CURE: TALK IT OVER

Friction between writers and their supervisors usually results from misunderstanding.

Both must form a smooth-working team to battle *fog*. They need to take time to consider and appreciate the other's viewpoint.

Granted, the pace of daily business doesn't allow for review of every document. Important reports, though, should be discussed before being composed. Occasional meetings about memos and letter writing, at which everyone can speak freely, can be helpful as well. When possible, follow these guidelines:

FOR SUPERVISORS

Don't insist that everyone working for you write the way you do. It's better to have each person do it his or her own way, but in harmony with the group.

If you must change another's writing, give the reasons why. Never say, "Because that's the way I want it." And make sure the writer understands your reasons.

FOR WRITERS

When you have an important piece to write, discuss it with your supervisor. Learn what to emphasize and what to downplay. This saves revision time.

Don't sulk about changes. Learn why they were made by reviewing them with the person responsible. Be thankful when revisions save you from making errors.

When possible, let the *writer* make the changes you want.

If you dislike having supervisors change your writing, remember: One way to prevent this from happening is to write so clearly that anyone would proudly sign your documents.

'WRITING' WRONGS

Below are some possible solutions to earlier exercises. They'll be most useful if you review them *after* you try your own revisions:

EXERCISE NO. 1 (PAGE 38):

The Sales Development Division is expected to:

• Advise in screening new products;

• Help select those that promise most profit;

• Conduct a development program for each new product until it reaches its top sales potential.

EXERCISE No. 2 (PAGE 42):

Here's a summary of plans, made at the June 22 meeting, for cutting costs of the spring sales campaign.

EXERCISE No. 3 (PAGE 44):

*Intra*division memos should be written as carefully as *inter*division ones. The practice helps improve your writing skills.

EXERCISE No. 4 (PAGE 62):

The Committee recommends that dinners be excluded from tuition refunds. This will reduce the refund from $560 to $455 if the tuition is paid in cash, or from $630 to $518 if paid in installments. This will bring the Refund Plan in line with the practices of other companies.

EXERCISE No. 5 (PAGE 70):

On August 17, you asked how we measure our bulk product deliveries. Report No. 334, dated September 27, 1982, describes the process. We still do it the same way.

THE 18 MOST COMMONLY ASKED QUESTIONS ABOUT BUSINESS WRITING

1. WHY DON'T I *ENJOY* WRITING?

Welcome to the club.

Business writing is rarely fun. In fact, it's safe to say that *most* writing done by most people isn't fun. Although diaries, journals, and some creative forms may be enjoyable, most writing challenges our organizational, reasoning, and inventive skills. Writing anything other than the simplest of messages can tax our concentration and patience.

The notion that writing should be enjoyable probably began in grade school when well-intentioned teachers sought to motivate us. Writing *could* be fun, they promised, once we knew enough about the craft to enjoy the experience. Unfortunately, they were wrong.

Worse, the "fun standard" trivializes the key requisite for good writing: hard work. Writing well requires time, energy, and a commitment to self-criticism and self-correction. The process can enlighten and gratify, but it's seldom fun. To think otherwise is to approach writing ill-prepared for its demands.

For most writers, "fun" comes from realizing that their efforts have produced a quality product, that they have communicated effectively and achieved their goal. Therein lies the writer's reward.

2. HOW CAN I WRITE FASTER?

Knowing *what* you want to say will help. Begin by *prewriting* — evaluating, selecting, and organizing your ideas — before starting your first draft.

Then try, as the saying goes, to *first get it written, then get it right!* In other words, finish the entire draft — no matter how rough it may be — before beginning detailed rewriting and editing.

Lingering over imperfect sentences before finishing your first draft stops the flow and rhythm of your thoughts. Too, you can correct a *completed* draft more effectively once you see all your ideas and where they fall. The whole reveals obvious flaws that are difficult to detect when they're segmented; also, you avoid reworking material you'll want to cut later, after seeing the whole.

Of course, nearly all the people we know complain that they write too slowly. Ironically, many excellent writers report that the time they spend on writing has actually increased as a result of their improved writing skills. Because they now recognize and appreciate good writing, they have higher standards to meet.

3. WHAT'S THE BEST WAY TO BEGIN AND ORGANIZE MOST MESSAGES?

Begin with your purpose — your bottom line. Put another way, what do you want your audience to know or do after they've read your message? State the answer in a *single, concise, active sentence* — not a question. This sentence is your *specific purpose*. Note that it's more precise than your *subject*, a broader area that usually doesn't include your viewpoint:

Subject: **staffing needs**

Specific Purpose: **We should hire two more accountants.**

Subject: **department meeting**

Specific Purpose: **The department meeting produced three goals.**

When appropriate, start your message with your specific purpose; otherwise, make sure it appears within your first paragraph.

Generally, state your specific purpose *before* elaborating on any introductory details, such as background information, definition of terms, or research methods. If you have more than one purpose, state them all before discussing any.

Ideally, each paragraph after your introduction should develop your purpose by developing *one* supporting point or topic. Summarize this point or topic in a "topic sentence" that begins the paragraph (the deductive pattern). All other sentences in the paragraph must relate to this point or topic.

One-sentence paragraphs are fine *if* they cover the entire point of the paragraph.

A good test of whether you've written a well-organized message with effective topic sentences is if it makes sense when you read only the first paragraph, coupled with the first sentence of each successive paragraph.

When giving "bad" news or reporting on delicate issues, however, you may want to lead up to your specific purpose. Follow the inductive pattern: Present your reasons, then state the conclusion supported. In this way, you don't appear insensitive — "Dear Karen: You're fired" — and you guard against initially upsetting the reader so that he or she stops after your first sentence before seeing your rationale.

4. SHOULD I ALWAYS SUMMARIZE AT THE END OF A MESSAGE?

Usually, it's a good idea — especially at the end of longer documents — to restate your purpose and summarize your main points. The reader may need to be reminded of your ideas; besides, a summary conclusion — the last thing read — drives your message home.

But it would be a mistake to see your conclusion as the *only* place to summarize. You can summarize also in the beginning or middle of your message. Or, you may not conclude with a summary (if your message is short, for example, or if you choose a more dramatic, illustrative closing). And you can summarize more than once.

Your introduction can summarize or "preview" what you *intend* to say. Previews focus the reader's attention by giving immediate structure to the text that follows. (They also help keep the writer on track.) Previews come usually at or near the introduction's end.

Internal summaries — brief summaries within the body of your message — can be used to review what you've said so far and what you're about to say: "In addition to Alison's computer skills and wide-ranging systems knowledge, another reason to hire her is that she speaks Chinese."

Some writers — overestimating their audience's ability to follow and retain long, often complex messages — dismiss summaries as obvious and unnecessary. Effective writers, meanwhile, know that comprehension soars when readers are given road signs indicating the territory covered and the trip remaining.

5. How should business documents be formatted?

Today, many businesses have their own ways of formatting documents. Templates that ensure consistency and professionalism are incorporated conveniently into the company's word-processing programs.

Without specific company guidelines, however, you'll choose from an array of memo, letter, and report formats. None of these is intrinsically "correct"; your selection simply reflects your taste and your needs.

But you should avoid uninviting, impractical extremes. Pick a format that's consistent, attractive, and readable. What *not* to do:

To: All employees of Red Eye Press

FROM: Mel Frank, Publisher
Date: March 18, 1994

SUBJECT: Robert Gunning Clear Writing Seminar

"FROM" and "SUBJECT" are all capitals, but "To" and "Date" aren't; entries are double-spaced, except between "FROM" and "Date"; and only "FROM" is boldface. Such inconsistencies reveal a general sloppiness and inattention to detail. The memo's overall appearance seems awkward and unbalanced.

Now consider this version:

TO: All Employees of Red Eye Press

FROM: Mel Frank, Publisher

DATE: March 18, 1994

SUBJECT: Robert Gunning Clear Writing Seminar

Notice how consistent (capitalized) headings, equally spaced lines, and blocked (post-colon) entries make this version clearer and easier to read.

6. WHEN COMMUNICATING *WITHIN* MY COMPANY, SHOULD I EVER SEND A LETTER INSTEAD OF A MEMO?

Most people consider a business letter more personal than a memo. After all, a letter usually begins with a salutation to one person. In contrast, a dozen people, on average, read a memo, according to Michael Markel in *Business Writing Essentials*.

In reality, of course, impersonal form letters and pervasive sales appeals dominate the mailways, while, in contrast, personal memos often address a specific reader, usually someone with whom the writer shares a long relationship.

Still, audiences *perceive* the letter form to be more personal and private than the popular memo, which symbolizes business communication. It's best, then, to send letters when imparting such personal information as special recognition and appreciation, promotions and demotions, formal invitations, and expressions of sympathy. By taking the extra time to compose a letter, you evoke the sense of a special message written by a caring person.

On the other hand, an external memo may seek a very different effect. Political and social action groups sometimes try to mobilize constituencies by redesigning standard request letters into "urgent" memos. The document then: (1) looks less like the usual appeal for resources; (2) implies that the issue(s) discussed is serious "business"; and (3) implicitly reminds group members that, despite their physical separation, they're a close (memo-sharing) collective that needs to act quickly.

7. Is it acceptable to refer to myself as 'I'?

Certainly "I" is preferable to "this writer," which is detached and stilted. And "I" allows for active-voice verbs whose subjects bear responsibility ("I hired Terri"), as opposed to passive-voice constructions devoid of responsible actors ("Terri was hired").

The use of "I," however, draws attention to the writer and swiftly personalizes any document. While that's beneficial at times, it can be problematic as well. It can undermine reports, proposals, or other documents that must convey an objective tone and the impression that the arguments and evidence presented speak for themselves.

Even in highly personalized memos and letters, excessive use of "I" and "me" may portray the writer as self-centered, egotistical, and overbearing. Here, too, "I" should be used carefully.

8. SHOULD I USE CONTRACTIONS?

Yes, especially in such informal documents as memos. Using contractions creates a natural, conversational tone to which readers better relate.

Clarity and emphasis, however, often demand the non-contracted form: "You shouldn't hire more staff" expresses less than "You should not hire more staff." ("Not" also allows for additional emphasis, i.e., *not* or **not**.) Similarly, "We'll do it" lacks the force of "We *will* do it." And can you even imagine Descartes saying, "I think, therefore I'm"?

Too, contractions should be avoided in formal documents. Here, convention calls for a more elevated style; contractions, abbreviations, colloquialisms, and exclamation marks seem out of place. In *Fumblerules*, William Safire writes:

You don't wear a tie to a ballgame, and you do not wear loafers to a church wedding. In the same way, you shouldn't use formal English when your intent is to be sassy and breezy, nor should you employ contractions in a solemn speech or formal letter.

Perhaps the ultimate value of contractions is that they seem to foster readable writing. Edward P. Bailey, in *The Plain English Approach to Business Writing*, contends that using contractions improves "write-ability" by inducing a conversational style that effects clearer, simpler sentences. Bailey suggests writing all the contents first with contractions to ensure readability, after which formal documents can be "*un*contracted."

9. Is there any harm in writing too informally?

Sometimes we're so confident about our subject or comfortable with our reader that we lose all restraint. Our writing becomes careless and unprofessional. Suddenly, because of a thoughtless word or phrase, we offend our reader.

More often, our informality leads to "shorthand" (undeveloped description and/or explanation) and hyperbole. We forget that our writing may be re-summoned by audiences having different backgrounds and agendas than our initial reader.

Shorthand, for example, poses a special problem. Abbreviated messages make full sense only to specific audiences at specific times. Such texts provide little help to successors, future employees, and others down the road. Only by having a clear and thorough corporate record to guide them can employees learn from the past. Without knowing what worked previously — *and how and why* — they're likely to reinvent existing wheels, duplicate projects, and repeat past mistakes.

Just as fatal is when shorthand or hyperbole legally exposes a company. Imagine, for instance, the ramifications of dismissing a longtime employee after a performance appraisal that read:

Chris has 10 times more problems with just about everything than any employee in the 200-year history of this company. Enough said.

Perhaps, but more *will* be said by Chris's lawyer.

10. WHEN IS IT APPROPRIATE TO USE THE PASSIVE VOICE?

In active voice, the subject *acts*; in passive voice, the subject receives the action or is *acted on*. Passive voice often leads to wordy, listless, and unclear prose. Still, the passive voice seems appropriate when:

The actor is not known.

> **The building was bombed.**
>
> **My dog was stolen.**

The actor is less important than the action.

> **My English teacher was fired.**
>
> **My writing class was canceled.**

The actor needs to be protected.

> **The requested files were delivered late.**
>
> **It was decided we'd all work late.**

You, the writer, want to sound objective and impersonal.

> **It's recommended, after careful consideration of the facts, that John be terminated.** (You want the facts to speak for themselves.)
>
> **Further, the conclusion supported by our investigation suggests that this action should have been taken long ago.**

You, the writer, want to vary your style.

After beginning three sentences on your job-application letter with "I" ("I supervised ... I managed ... I directed ..."), you decide to limit your "I's":

> **A new corporate sales brochure was also designed and completed.**

11. Should I avoid using gender-specific pronouns?

Most people have come to recognize gender-specific pronouns (he/she; him/her; his/hers) as sexist and stereotypical. They limit role modeling by implicitly championing one gender over the other. As such, their use may alienate some readers. Fortunately, gender-specific pronouns can be easily changed:

Pluralize singular subjects.

> **Each staff member must submit <u>his</u> travel request.** vs.: **Staff member<u>s</u> must submit <u>their</u> travel requests.**

If you want to emphasize the individual, here are some other options:

Cut or change unnecessary pronouns.

> **The manager was limited by <u>his</u> company budget.** vs.: **The manager was limited by the company budget.**

> **Each staff member must submit <u>his</u> travel request.** vs.: **Each staff member must submit <u>a</u> travel request.**

> Or, if an informal tone will do: **<u>You</u> need to submit <u>your</u> travel request.**

Restructure the sentence.

> Instead of: **Every consultant should be computer literate if <u>he</u> expects to be hired,** write: **Every consultant who expects to be hired should be computer literate.**

Use "he/she" or "he or she."

Sometimes only "he/she" or "he or she" will do. These are a bit wordier, but they work if used sparingly. "S/he" is more economical, although its appeal still seems limited, because it's confusing to read.

Try alternating gender-specific pronouns.

Use "him" for one example; use "her" for another. You'll shed the baggage of "he/she," although you may disorient some readers used to a single, gender-consistent subject.

Another tactic now becoming popular — which we *don't* recommend — is to go ahead and use plural pronouns, even when their referent nouns are singular: "Each staff member should submit their travel request." Better, more creative solutions exist than simply ignoring grammatical rules and the logic of our language.

12. How can I write clearly and still minimize legal exposure?

Many business writers attempt to minimize legal exposure by resorting to what they think is a legal style. They qualify every statement with long, convoluted sentences that consume the reader's time and effort. Yet, the prose doesn't necessarily protect the writer or the company.

Generally, business writers think only of their *immediate* audience. They forget that another, *future* audience — a legal audience — may one day read their messages as well. To write clearly and still be "legally correct," business writers must first recognize how this audience — which includes lawyers, jurors, and judges — think about business documents:

• Courts consider business documents to have *limited* confidentiality. In litigation, most company information must be disclosed to all parties — and even to the public, if a trial ensues. Those who believe that personal memos and private records can't be subpoenaed may be surprised.

• Trial attorneys will scrutinize all documents and then try to use them to prove their cases. Thus, anything you write can serve purposes *unintended* by you.

• Trial attorneys will distort business documents and refer to them out of context. It's not unusual for attorneys to generalize from but *one* in a series of reports (the others having been lost or destroyed).

• Courts view all business documents — and the employees who create them — as representing a company's knowledge and attitudes.

• In judicial proceedings, *written* business documents are considered more reliable than *oral* statements.

These guidelines can help legally protect your business writing without swelling your prose:

• Define important terms and use them precisely and consistently. If you don't, others can argue that any variation was intended and that different terms mean different things.

• Use legal, business, and industry- or profession-specific terms properly. When discussing a product problem, for example, describe the *problem*; resist offhanded conclusions that the product is "defective," a term having significant legal implications in product-liability cases.

• Stay within your expertise, offer opinions prudently, and label each one so it isn't taken as fact.

• Support your claims with evidence — facts, examples, statistics, and testimony.

• Avoid using absolute statements. Once you say "It never happens," it will. Often you need only change a word or add a simple qualifier to stand on safer ground, i.e., "It rarely happens."

• Limit use of "colorful" language. Marketing departments frequently use fighting language to motivate their salespeople. However, when this language finds its way into antitrust litigation, it's taken out of context to establish a company's intent to monopolize.

- When in doubt about what to write, or when writing about a topic that clearly has legal implications, seek legal advice.

13. Why do readers often misunderstand me, even when I write clearly?

Your writing always will seem clearer to you than to anyone else. Because *you* know what you want to say, you *mentally* connect and transition your thoughts in ways that readers won't. Hence, it's what you *don't* say that creates confusion.

Even a well-organized message can be hard to follow if you don't label what you're doing. Help your reader by providing cues.

Tell when you're giving your purpose. Write: "I propose . . . "; "I contend . . . "; "This memo outlines . . . "; or "We'll describe . . . " For added clarity, underline, italicize, or boldface your purpose statement.

Tell when you're introducing a major point. If you have three points, for example, designate each: "My first point . . . A second point . . . My final point . . . " Or: (1) Number or letter your points [1, 2, 3; or (a), (b), (c)]; (2) Underline, italicize, boldface, or bullet the first sentence introducing each point; or (3) Make each point into a heading that tops the discussion. In short, label your main points, both verbally and visually.

Tell when you're comparing and contrasting. Readers will follow your analysis better if you mark important comparisons and contrasts with reinforcing phrases, such as:

Although . . .	Much like . . .
As opposed to . . .	On the other hand . . .
Identical to . . .	Rather than . . .
In contrast to . . .	Similar to . . .
Meanwhile . . .	Whereas . . .

Tell when you're drawing a conclusion. Introduce conclusions by reviewing how they result: "The mixture of 'A' and 'B', as I've described, produces 'C'." Or, consider just prefacing your conclusion ("'C' occurs . . .") with:

Accordingly . . .

Consequently . . .

Hence . . .

Therefore . . .

Thus . . .

Tell when you're summarizing. Use a heading, if appropriate, or simply write:

Finally . . .

In conclusion . . .

In short . . .

In sum . . .

In summary . . .

Last . . .

Overall . . .

14. WHAT SHOULD I DO WHEN I'M GIVEN A WRITING SAMPLE THAT I SENSE IS FLAWED, BUT I DON'T KNOW EXACTLY WHAT'S WRONG OR HOW TO FIX IT?

Your instincts are probably correct. Usually such a sample *is* flawed, even though *you* can't identify why.

However, if you compare what the writer promises to what's actually delivered (and how), you'll realize the problem is often organizational: Ideas don't follow one another, or they're developed out of sequence.

Begin by briefly outlining the entire message as it appears. Jot down the purpose found in the first paragraph (the promise) and the main point of each paragraph (the delivery). When you finish, review your outline. The possible problem may now emerge: An argument raised in one place is discussed in another; a section having several points develops only some; or a key idea receives sporadic, inconsistent attention.

If you still can't find what's wrong, go back and flesh out your outline. This time, include how each point is specifically supported.

This approach can't identify every writing problem, but it does help pinpoint many common structural flaws.

15. HOW CAN I USE MY COMPUTER TO WRITE BETTER?

Computers can improve your writing in many ways:

Prewriting. Taking notes on a computer is faster than writing them by hand. Moreover, a computer provides rapid, portable (via diskette) access to those notes. They can also be outlined with word-processing templates, or organized more rigorously by database applications.

Composing. When you compose at the computer, you write and rewrite almost simultaneously; both become a single, unified activity wherein thought and expression more closely match. And because text can be compared and changed so easily, you "experiment" far more than you would if the text were "fixed" (done on an old-fashioned typewriter) and every major change meant retyping the entire manuscript.

Just as your "first" draft emerges more refined, subsequent drafts benefit as much when rewritten and edited on a computer. You can quickly compare several versions of any sentence or passage and make changes without penalty. This ease of moving and transposing text encourages confidence, creativity, and new ways of thinking about writing. Composition becomes a friendlier, less menacing process that invites participation.

Editing. Computers help you polish your work by speedily checking your spelling and (to some degree) grammar. The computer can check also for repeated word use. This feature, when combined with a thesaurus program, is particularly helpful in spotting and avoiding repetitious language. Editing can benefit further from computer networking, E-mail, and faxing, which make it easier for you to circulate drafts for review by others.

Formatting. Computers (together with printers and software) feature numerous formatting options that promote readability. Besides providing a variety of scalable typefaces, computers allow for italics, boldfacing, small caps, justified margins, double columns, and a host of other simple graphics. These *tools* can't produce good writing, but they can render well-written messages even more compelling.

16. When is it Best Not to Write a Memo or Letter?

Some people want a written record of everything they say and do; others seek the reverse. The best strategy probably lies somewhere in the middle: Think always of documenting work performance, but know when it's best *not* to record your words and deeds. Here are some examples:

When You're Angry. Granted, some passion is needed to give vigor and soul to your writing. But when you're furious, you'll likely say things that only worsen the problem and cause regret.

Equally harmful, the *tone* of such memos and letters can negatively affect your image and credibility. That's especially true when outbursts, immortalized by written records, are saved by savvy foes.

When You're Conveying Highly Personal or Sensitive Information. Sometimes anything other than an oral, face-to-face meeting seems cold and removed. You wouldn't end a marriage by telegram, so why use E-mail to bid farewell to a longtime, loyal employee?

Effective business communicators reflect an aura of character and decency. They care enough about their audience to sense when only human contact will do. So, when Gary and Mary get drunk at the company picnic and loudly insult one another, their supervisors know to *talk* to them once they're sober. But if Gary and Mary *arrive* at work drunk, that's another, more serious matter. Even when highly personal or sensitive matters require written record, they can also be discussed orally.

When You're Facing Time-Consuming Writing. Some memos and letters take forever, particularly when you're asked to explain complex material or answer several lengthy questions. In these cases (excepting legal requests), it's often faster to *talk* to the people involved. Information can be questioned and clarified immediately, thus minimizing the need for follow-up memos and letters. If written record is needed, you can summarize the conversation.

When You're Speaking Off the Record. If you want to communicate off the record, why record it? Privately express your position orally, or consider not expressing it at all.

17. HOW LONG SHOULD I KEEP COPIES OF MY MEMOS AND LETTERS?

Keeping copies of all memos and letters proves impractical and unnecessary. But discarding them prematurely can be unwise — and even risky. A better approach takes case-by-case action based upon legal requirements and company needs.

Legal requirements take two forms:

(a) Federal laws (and sometimes state statutes) prescribe how long certain records — especially those regarding tax, securities, employment, health and safety, and environmental matters — should be kept. Additional governmental record-keeping guidelines apply to several specific industries, such as banking, transportation, health care, and mass media.

(b) Legal proceedings often require written proofs. Effective record keeping can aid these proceedings, or even prevent some from occurring. A typical example features the familiar battle over ownership rights that evolves because of insufficient proof of title.

Company needs include a complete history of operating procedures and key corporate events. Without such, you're less likely to conduct business as conveniently and efficiently as possible. Nor can you provide accurate, full disclosure of all pertinent facts upon future sale of the company. By destroying vital company history, then, you lessen both the success and value of your business.

Nonvital documents, however, needn't be saved beyond a reasonable time period. Copies of meeting announcements, simple transmittal letters, and drafts of completed work, for example, require only a short retention period insofar as any issues or questions they raise occur soon after they're created.

18. Why should I learn to write clearly if it only makes it easier to blame me later when something goes wrong?

It's true that a well-written message can be a double-edged sword. Whenever you clearly state a position, it's more accessible to criticism. And when you take clear responsibility for that position, you leave yourself open for potential blame. Hence, some writers deliberately muddle everything they say, hoping neither the "act" nor the "actor" is quite clear. Ambiguity, they believe, will leave them enough maneuvering room to later claim credit or deny fault.

Sadly, some companies *do* encourage slippery, oily writing by scapegoating failure and looking always to blame. Until they change, it's useless to ask their employees to write clearly; *fog* is their survival tool.

Good writing starts at the top. Management must not only champion clear expression, it must also commit to a corporate culture that endorses it. It must nurture initiative and encourage responsibility by acting fairly and realistically.

Finally, we're obligated to concede that *knowing* how to write clearly helps even those choosing *not to* do so. Once you know enough about writing to compose clearly, you know also enough to be vague. Similar to the visual artist who understands perspective well enough to challenge it, the business writer who masters clarity can, if necessary, purposely create ambiguity.

COMPLETE YOUR MANAGEMENT LIBRARY WITH THESE DARTNELL BOOKS

THE CUSTOMER SERVICE REP'S SURVIVAL GUIDE SERIES FROM DARTNELL

Have you ever thought how many businesses lose money because customer service reps are not properly versed in the fine art of dealing with people? **The Customer Service Rep's Survival Guide Series** is a quick and easy way to motivate and train customer service reps to perform their best!

Completely unpretentious, the guides are written and illustrated for quick and easy reading. The guides also have a serious message—to teach your customer service team practical tips, inspiration, and insights into human nature. Whether they work with two customers a day or 200; your reps will improve the relationship your company has with all its customers. And that adds up to increased sales.

TOUGH CUSTOMERS: HOW TO KEEP THEM SMILING . . . AND YOURSELF SANE!

This book teaches the front line how to deal with tough customers. Specifically, problem solving and handling unique situations as they arise. Topics include:

- Dealing with difficult customers, including keeping cool under pressure.
- Problem prevention—Is the customer always right?
- Serving customers according to needs, giving special care to older customers, children, and disabled customers.

150 pages; paperback; $10.95
Book Code: 8124

STANDOUT SERVICE TALK STRAIGHT, THINK POSITIVE, AND SMILE!

The first volume is the basics, emphasizing attitude and courtesy to customers. Topics include:

- What is customer service?
- Recognizing customers' needs and providing timely service.
- How technology can improve your skills—including using the fax machine and voice mail.

150 pages; paperback; $10.95
Book code: 8123

THE EXTRA MILE: BUILDING PROFITABLE CUSTOMER RELATIONS EVERY TIME

This book is designed to show how to go the extra distance with every customer encounter:

- Evaluating customer needs through critical questioning.
- Transforming the order taker into the customer sales rep through cross-selling and building repeat business.
- Encouraging a companywide commitment to service and improving lines of communication.

150 pages; paperback; $10.95
Book Code: 8122

TELEPHONE TERRIFIC! FACTS, FUN, AND 103 PRACTICAL TIPS FOR PHONE SUCCESS

Whether you're a customer service rep, salesperson, secretary, receptionist, telemarketer, or just anyone who conducts business over the phone, **Telephone Terrific!** will help you to brush up on the basics; to handle tricky situations; to think on your feet (and on the phone); and, through humorous and historical looks at telephones and the people who use them, to take the tough times less seriously.

- More than 100 helpful Quick Tips—helpful ideas and suggestions for better communication skills—throughout the book.
- Close-up interviews with telephone pros—take a stroll through the nostalgic past; learn how the pros keep up with technology, define customer satisfaction, and more.
- Test your skills—each chapter ends with a quiz so you can test and sharpen your skills.

150 pages; paperback; $8.95 each
Book code: 8492

T.E.A.M.S: TOGETHER EACH ACHIEVES MORE SUCCESS
BY JIM LUNDY

Jim Lundy, author of *Lead, Follow, or Get Out of the Way*, takes readers step-by-step through assessing their own companies' needs and setting goals; scouting outstanding talent; improving leadership skills; making sure that employees and managers are communicating; and tracking performance and productivity. This guide's farseeing practical information gives everyone the tools to build a superior team from the ground up. Using actual cases, this book provides you with:

- Sores of checklists and outlines to improve team effectiveness and efficiency.
- Winning strategies for improved interdepartmental communication, coordination, and cooperation.
- Proven guidelines for conflict resolution.

230 pages; hardcover; $19.95; Book code: 1207

THE PROFESSIONAL SECRETARY'S SURVIVAL GUIDE

More than ever, your company's secretaries and other office support staff must know the most productive, effective shortcuts, timesavers, and costcutters.

More than ever, they need the "people skills" to work productively with fellow employees, to handle tough customer or clients, and to answer every question that comes their way.

Secretaries make a vital contribution to the "big picture" every day in your office — and to your company's success! Help your secretaries help you . . . by giving each of them this one-of-a-kind sourcebook of the best proven tips, tales, advice, and guidelines for office success. Your company's office teams will benefit immediately from The Survival Guide's:

- Shortcuts for boosting productivity on the computer, telephone, and fax machine.
- Tips for cost control, time, and paper savings.
- Humorous quotes and stories for building effective communication.
- Quizzes to rate and sharpen office and people skills, and more!

159 pages; paperback; $6.95 each Book code: 8120
